BIRDSEYE
WRITING SKILLS: SENTENCES

BEVERLEY DIETZ

Fearon Teacher Aids
a division of
Pitman Learning, Inc.
Belmont, California

Editorial director: Ina Tabibian
Editor: Robin Kelly
Illustrator: Bill Eral
Design director: Eleanor Mennick
Production editor: Anne Lewis
Manufacturing manager: Susan Siegel

Birdseye and other characters developed by Beverly Cory

ISBN-0-8224-0722-1
Library of Congress Catalog Card Number: 83-62441
Printed in the United States of America.
1. 9 8 7 6 5 4 3 2 1

CONTENTS

CONTENTS *continued*

HIDDEN TREASURE

Suzanna always speaks in *whole sentences*. Each group of words she says expresses a complete thought. She tells who or what she is talking about and then tells something about it. Her cousin Sue doesn't speak in whole sentences. Suzanna and Sue have a dog named Scamp. Scamp doesn't speak at all.

One day, Suzanna, Sue, and Scamp went on a hunt for hidden treasure. Read the word groups that tell about their hunt. Underline each whole sentence that Suzanna might have said.

1. An old map with a big red X in one corner.

2. Scamp carried it in his mouth to Suzanna and Sue.

3. The map was a complete surprise to the two girls.

4. Looking for hidden treasure.

5. Someplace right in their own garden.

6. They watched Scamp's tail.

7. The tool collection from the garage included two shovels for the girls to use.

8. The sight of Scamp sniffing the ground made them enthusiastic.

9. Followed the crooked lines of the map.

10. The two girls and their dog.

11. Suddenly sat down in a corner of the vegetable garden.

12. A wonderful buried treasure must be right there!

13. Dug together for a long time.

14. Even their bones began to feel tired.

Is it a chest of gold?

What was the hidden treasure? Write the third word from each sentence you underlined.

_____

Birdseye Writing Skills: Sentences copyright © 1983 Pitman Learning, Inc.

BONNIE AND HER BOXES

Bonnie Boxer likes to put *everything* into boxes. She even puts sentences into boxes. She puts each kind of sentence into a different box. She puts sentences that tell something into a box marked **statements**. She puts sentences that ask something into a box marked **questions**. She puts sentences that tell someone to do something into a box marked **commands**. She puts sentences that express strong feeling into a box marked **exclamations**.

Help Bonnie put these sentences into boxes. Read each sentence. Then write its number in the correct box below.

1. I keep everything I own in boxes.

2. Boxes are so much fun!

3. Please put these boxes back on the shelf.

4. Does anyone know where I put that box of goldfish?

5. I can't remember where it is.

6. Look up there.

7. Isn't something dripping out of the box on top?

8. Did you put water into the box of goldfish?

9. Of course I did!

10. All goldfish live in water.

11. The water must be leaking out of the box!

12. Bring the goldfish some more water.

I think we found them just in time!

STATEMENTS

QUESTIONS

COMMANDS

EXCLAMATIONS

Skill: Identifying kinds of sentences.

BIRDSEYE'S FRIENDS AT WORK

Birdseye has four friends. Each friend uses only one kind of sentence.

Stacey uses only **statements**. All her sentences tell something.

Quentin uses only **questions**. All his sentences ask something.

Cory uses only **commands**. All his sentences tell someone to do something.

Exeter uses only **exclamations**. All his sentences express strong feelings.

Read each sentence, and decide which of Birdseye's friends said it. Then write **statement**, **question**, **command**, or **exclamation** to tell which kind of sentence it is.

1. I have the plans right here. _____

2. Let me see them. _____

3. What a great place this will be! _____

4. Don't we need a few more windows? _____

5. Where is the dining room? _____

6. It will have a great view! _____

7. We should start working right away. _____

8. Bring the hammer and some nails. _____

9. This is hard work! _____

10. You almost dropped the board on my foot. _____

11. You were in the way. _____

12. Isn't anybody else tired? _____

13. Don't start complaining. _____

14. Why isn't Birdseye helping us? _____

> When my friends finish working, I'll visit them in their new house.

Birdseye Writing Skills: Sentences copyright © 1983 Pitman Learning, Inc.

Skill: Identifying kinds of sentences.

WANDERING WOODY

Birdseye has a neighbor named Wandering Woody who often does some very silly things. Birdseye and her friends like to write notes to each other about Wandering Woody. Sometimes they forget to put *punctuation marks* at the end of their sentences. They forget to follow these guidelines:
—Use a period at the end of every statement.
—Use a question mark at the end of every question.
—Use a period at the end of every command.
—Use an exclamation point if you want the sentence to show strong feeling.

Help Birdseye and her friends with their notes. Add a punctuation mark at the end of each sentence.

1. Can you guess where I saw Wandering Woody last night

2. He was in the fireplace

3. I saw him there, too

4. What was Woody doing in the fireplace

5. He lay down in the fireplace so he could sleep like a log

6. Have you seen Wandering Woody today

7. He looks terribly worried

8. What's bothering him

9. He has to have a blood test this afternoon, and he hasn't finished studying for it

10. Guess where Wandering Woody was last week

11. I saw him standing at the top of a tall ladder

12. He stands up there because he wants to join the school chorus

13. How is standing on a ladder going to help him

14. Wandering Woody thinks it will help him hit the high notes

Birdseye Writing Skills: Sentences copyright © 1983 Pitman Learning, Inc.

Skill: Punctuating sentences.

PICKING UP THE PIECES

Careless Carla found some boxes full of sentences. Poor Carla always drops things, and of course she dropped the boxes. Now the sentences are all mixed up.

Help Careless Carla put the sentences back together. Rearrange the words in each group to form the right kind of sentence. Remember to add the correct punctuation mark at the end of each sentence.

Statements

1. I to love baseball play

   _____

2. play on I a team Sluggers called the

   _____

3. will win The Sluggers the championship this season

   _____

Questions

4. you like Do baseball to play

   _____

5. What do position you play

   _____

6. you Would to practice with like us

   _____

Commands

7. the Watch ball

   _____

8. as as hard Hit it you can

   _____

Exclamations

9. What hit a great that was

   _____

10. should You the Sluggers join

    _____

AT THE BEACH

Birdseye and her friends spent the day at the beach. These pictures show what they did there, but some sentences are missing from each picture. Write what the characters might say. The label under the speaker tells you what *kind* of sentence to write.

1.

2.

3.

Birdseye Writing Skills: Sentences copyright © 1983 Pitman Learning, Inc.

Skill: Writing sentences.

SPELUNKING WITH SPENCER

Spencer is a spelunker. That means he likes to explore caves. Spencer and his friends often see unusual plants and special rocks in caves. Once, they saw an unusual animal.

Underline the *subject* of each sentence. Then circle the answer that tells how many words are in the sentence subject. The first sentence has been done as an example.

1. <u>Spencer</u> explored a cave last weekend. (a. 1) b. 2

2. A range of rocky mountains is not far from his home. r. 3 s. 5

3. Several small, dark caves are located in those mountains. m. 4 n. 6

4. They are very interesting to spelunkers like Spencer. a. 1 b. 3

5. Three other spelunkers explored the cave with Spencer. k. 2 l. 3

6. All the explorers carried flashlights. l. 3 m. 4

7. The spelunkers heard a strange flapping sound near the back of the cave. a. 1 b. 2

8. Spencer shined his light there. a. 1 b. 2

9. The bright light from the flashlight frightened the animal. s. 3 t. 6

What did Spencer and the other spelunkers see? Write the letter from each answer you circled above.

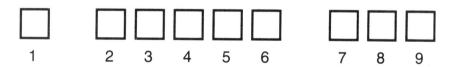

| 1 | | 2 | 3 | 4 | 5 | 6 | | 7 | 8 | 9 |

It wasn't a dragon, was it?

Birdseye Writing Skills: Sentences copyright © 1983 Pitman Learning, Inc.

Skill: Identifying sentence subjects.

WELCOME TO THE ZOO

At the zoo, Birdseye noticed something strange. The subject of each sentence was missing from the zoo animal signs. Finish each sign by adding a sentence subject that makes sense.

1 _____ once lived in the jungles of Africa.

2 _____ can hang by their long tails.

3 _____ perform tricks every day at two o'clock.

4 _____ can be poisonous.

5 _____ cannot fly.

6 _____ have huge jaws with sharp teeth.

7 _____ can see in the dark.

Why isn't there a sign about me?

Skill: Adding sentence subjects.

THE NOUN-NAPPER

This poor fuzzy monster is sad because it has no name. Since the monster doesn't have a name of its own, it collects naming words, or *nouns*. The monster collects nouns like **bird** and **bicycle**. It also collects special names, called *proper nouns*, such as **Birdseye** and **Scamp**.

The monster has collected all the nouns from the subjects of these sentences. In place of each noun, the monster has left a string of n's. Cross out each string of n's, and put back the noun you think the monster took.

1. A fierce nnnnnn has been following me.

2. Those two nnnnnn are singing beautifully.

3. Nnnnnn was sneaking silently away.

4. Our nnnnnn waved cheerfully to us.

5. Three friendly nnnnnn were running and jumping outside.

6. Only nnnnnn is still here.

7. Suddenly, the graceful nnnnnn tripped and fell.

8. My favorite nnnnnn was waiting outside.

9. The huge nnnnnn stopped unexpectedly.

10. Nnnnnn and nnnnnn laughed about it together.

11. The big nnnnnn and the little nnnnnn chased each other.

12. All your nnnnnn made me laugh.

Give the sad monster a name of its own. Since the monster's special name will be a proper noun, it must start with a

capital letter. _____

Birdseye Writing Skills: Sentences copyright © 1983 Pitman Learning, Inc.

Skill: Adding sentence subject nouns.

OLLIE OUTDO

Birdseye has a friend named Ollie Outdo. Ollie always has to have more of everything than his friends have. If Birdseye has one **bike**, Ollie wants two **bikes**. If Birdseye has one **pony**, Ollie must have at least two **ponies**. And if Birdseye eats one **batch** of cookies, Ollie must eat three or four **batches**!

Finish these sentences about Birdseye and Ollie. Add a plural noun in each blank space.

1. Birdseye has one little brother. Ollie has two little _____.

2. Birdseye has one older sister. Ollie has three older _____.

3. Birdseye has one pet mouse. Ollie has six pet _____.

4. Birdseye sees one bright orange butterfly. Ollie sees three bright

    orange _____.

5. Birdseye has one guppy. Ollie has ten _____.

6. Birdseye has one best friend. Ollie has two best _____.

7. Birdseye takes care of one rosebush. Ollie takes care of

    four _____.

8. Birdseye has one good idea. Ollie has three good _____.

9. Birdseye lives near one library. Ollie lives near two _____.

10. Birdseye has visited one foreign country. Ollie has visited four

    foreign _____.

11. Birdseye went to see one movie. Ollie went to see

    two _____.

12. Birdseye ate one peach. Ollie ate three _____.

13. Birdseye talked with one woman. Ollie talked with

    two _____.

14. Birdseye has one new watch. Ollie has two new _____.

Skill: Using plural noun forms (including common irregulars).

POLLY PARROT

Polly Parrot has just learned to talk. She repeats every sentence that Birdseye says. However, in place of the sentence subject Birdseye uses, Polly uses one of the *personal pronouns* in the box.

he	she	it	we	they

Read each sentence Birdseye says. Then write the sentence the way Polly Parrot would repeat it. Use a personal pronoun in place of the subject of Birdseye's sentence.

1. *Birdseye:* The Crofts lost their famous diamond.

   Polly: _____

2. *Birdseye:* Sheila Spy was asked to solve the mystery.

   Polly: _____

3. *Birdseye:* Donald Detective was assigned to help her.

   Polly: _____

4. *Birdseye:* The case was a very difficult assignment.

   Polly: _____

5. *Birdseye:* The clues were hard to understand.

   Polly: _____

6. *Birdseye:* The diamond was extremely valuable.

   Polly: _____

7. *Birdseye:* Sheila and Donald worked very hard.

   Polly: _____

8. *Birdseye:* You and I could have helped them solve the case.

   Polly: _____

Birdseye Writing Skills: Sentences copyright © 1983 Pitman Learning, Inc.

TILLIE AND TWEEZLE

Tillie and Tweezle like to do everything together. For that reason, they like sentences with *compound subjects*. Each sentence that they like has two subjects joined by the conjunction **and**.

Help Tillie and Tweezle find the sentences they like. Underline each sentence that has a compound subject.

1. Tillie and Tweezle practice skating every day.

2. Their coach helps them.

3. Their parents and their friends encourage them.

4. Tillie enjoys skating backwards most of all.

5. Tweezle considers jumps the best part of skating.

6. Tillie and Tweezle entered their first skating competition.

7. They felt quite nervous.

8. The skaters and the judges gathered near the ice.

9. One judge explained the rules of the competition.

10. Another judge and her partner gave some examples.

11. The skaters and the people in the audience clapped for the judges.

12. Tillie's friend Iona entered the competition, too.

13. Iona and her brother Ike skated first.

14. They skated very well together.

15. Tillie and Tweezle congratulated their friends.

It looks so easy!

Birdseye Writing Skills: Sentences copyright © 1983 Pitman Learning, Inc.

Skill: Identifying compound subjects.

MS. MATCHETT'S MACHINE

Ms. Matchett gets tired of saying or writing two sentences when one sentence is enough. So she has invented a special machine called the Sentence Squeezer. It combines two sentences into one.

Ms. Matchett has programmed the Sentence Squeezer to make sentences with compound subjects. Read the sentence pairs. Run them through the Sentence Squeezer. Write a new sentence for each pair, using a compound subject.

1. Lottie went camping. Her friends went camping.

   _____

2. Lottie pitched the tent. Doreen pitched the tent.

   _____

3. Jan gathered wood for the campfire. Nina gathered wood for the campfire.

   _____

4. Anya started cooking dinner. Her mother started cooking dinner.

   _____

5. The hamburgers tasted great. The roasted marshmallows tasted great.

   _____

6. The tall mountains were beautiful. The clear lakes were beautiful.

   _____

7. Beth wanted to go hiking. Peter wanted to go hiking.

   _____

8. Tom went fishing instead of hiking. Heidi went fishing instead of hiking.

   _____

Birdseye Writing Skills: Sentences copyright © 1983 Fitman Learning, Inc.

BIRDSEYE'S SPECIAL CIRCUS

Birdseye decided to put together a local circus performance. All of her friends wanted to be in the circus. There were so many performers that they had to work in pairs. Look at the picture of Birdseye's circus. Then fill in the blanks to finish the sentences about the circus performers. Each sentence will have a compound subject.

Step right up for a great performance under the Birdseye Big Top!

1. _____ and _____ juggled.

2. _____ and _____ walked on the tightrope.

3. _____ and _____ jumped through a hoop.

4. _____ and _____ pedaled their unicycles.

5. _____ and _____ swung from the trapeze.

6. _____ and _____ rode on a big horse.

Birdseye Writing Skills: Sentences copyright © 1983 Pitman Learning, Inc.

Skill: Adding compound subjects.

PENELOPE'S PETS

Penelope loves animals, and she has some unusual pets. Penelope tries to take very good care of her pets. Sometimes, though, Penelope and her pets act a little silly.

Read these sentences about Penelope and her pets. Circle the *predicate* of each sentence. Remember that the predicate tells what the sentence subject does or is or has.

1. A little yellow duck is one of Penelope's favorite pets.

2. The little duck felt sick one day.

3. The duck's bill looked pale.

4. Its feathers drooped.

5. Penelope wanted to help her sick duck.

6. The doctor wouldn't take care of Penelope's duck.

7. Penelope called a quack instead.

8. Penelope has a pet frog, too.

9. This frog is an excellent jumper.

10. It can jump higher than the Empire State Building.

11. The Empire State Building can't jump very high at all.

12. Another of Penelope's pets is a big watchdog.

13. Penelope has trained her dog very carefully.

14. The dog still runs around in circles, though.

15. The dog must be trying to wind itself up.

Birdseye Writing Skills: Sentences copyright © 1983 Pitman Learning, Inc.

Skill: Identifying sentence predicates.

SPORTS CONFUSION

Joe Jumble and his sister Jill worked together to write these sports sentences. Joe wrote the subject and Jill wrote the predicate of each sentence. Before they finished, though, they jumbled all the sentence parts together.

Match the subjects and predicates in these lists. Choose the best predicate for each subject. Then write the six sentences that Joe and Jill might have written.

Subjects	**Predicates**
All the players on our team	cheered for the players after the game.
The coach	shouted to the players.
The soccer game	ran onto the playing field.
The people in the stands	started at noon.
A big bulldog	blocked every kick.
The goalie from the other team	acted as our team mascot.

1. _____

_____

2. _____

_____

3. _____

_____

4. _____

_____

5. _____

_____

6. _____

_____

Birdseye Writing Skills: Sentences copyright © 1983 Pitman Learning, Inc.

Skill: Matching sentence subjects and predicates.

A SURPRISE PARTY

Lupe and Diego wanted to do something special for their mother's birthday. The pictures below show what they did, but the predicates are missing from the sentences beside the pictures. Finish each sentence by writing a predicate.

Birthday parties are for the birds.

1. Lupe _____
   _____
   _____

2. Her brother _____
   _____
   _____

3. Lupe _____
   _____
   _____

4. Diego _____
   _____
   _____

5. All the guests _____
   _____
   _____

6. Their mother _____
   _____
   _____

Skill: Writing sentence predicates.

LAZY LEONA

Leona is unbelievably lazy! Whenever possible, Leona avoids all action. She even avoids *verbs*, which are usually action words.

To help Leona overcome her laziness, Birdseye has added verbs to Leona's sentences. In each sentence, circle the verb that Birdseye added.

1. The sun rises early.

2. I stay in bed until noon.

3. I walk slowly toward my favorite tree.

4. I talk to the tree for a moment.

5. Then I lie down under the tree.

6. My afternoon nap ends after three or four hours.

7. The other animals move noisily through the jungle.

8. The monkeys chatter in the trees.

9. The elephants stroll toward the pond.

10. A happy bird flies in circles above me.

11. A huge gorilla munches bananas.

12. The zebras trot happily together.

What is Leona's favorite activity? To answer this question, match the number under each box with the number in the list of Leona's sentences. Find the first letter of the verb in that sentence, and write the letter in the box.

Leona likes to ☐ ☐ ☐ ☐
           1 6 2 4

Skill: Identifying verbs.

BEST FRIENDS

Nick and Vinnie are best friends, but they disagree about almost everything. They even disagree about words. Nick says **radio** is a noun, and Vinnie says **radio** is a verb. Read what Nick and Vinnie are saying. You'll see that they're both right!

Here are some words Nick and Vinnie disagree about. Read the two sentences in each pair, and add a word from the box to finish each sentence in a meaningful way. Then write **N** after the sentence if the word is used as a noun, or naming word. Write **V** after the sentence if the word is used as a verb, or word showing action.

| pedal | star | cheer | sign | lights | dress |

1. The _____ of the show was a talking horse. _____

   Two new actors _____ in that TV show. _____

2. The cyclists _____ up the steep hill. _____

   The brake _____ is below the steering wheel. _____

3. Dad _____ the candles on the birthday cake. _____

   The _____ went out during the storm. _____

4. The _____ said that the store was closed. _____

   Both witnesses _____ the papers. _____

5. A celebration brings _____ and happiness. _____

   When Nancy is unhappy, her friends _____ her up. _____

6. The young children _____ themselves. _____

   Mom's new _____ is bright red. _____

Birdseye Writing Skills: Sentences copyright © 1983 Pitman Learning, Inc.

Skill: Distinguishing nouns and verbs.

MORE DISAGREEMENTS

Nick and Vinnie are still disagreeing. Nick says that **play** is a noun, and Vinnie says that **play** is a verb. Which friend is right?

Nick and Vinnie disagree about the words in the box. Read the two sentences in each pair, and add a word from the box to finish each sentence. Then write **N** after the sentence if the word is used as a noun, or naming word. Write **V** after the sentence if the word is used as a verb, or word showing action.

form	step	store	wave	fish	time

1. The friends _____ their hands in the air. _____

   A huge _____ crashed onto the beach. _____

2. The passengers _____ carefully off the bus. _____

   Who was standing on the top _____? _____

3. A large silver _____ swam down the river. _____

   Many people _____ from this bridge. _____

4. Two officials _____ every race. _____

   The _____ is exactly two o'clock. _____

5. What _____ should I fill out to enter the contest? _____

   The baker must _____ the bread dough into a braided

   shape. _____

6. The _____ will be open until nine tonight. _____

   They _____ the old clothes in their attic. _____

Birdseye Writing Skills: Sentences copyright © 1983 Pitman Learning, Inc.

Skill: Distinguishing nouns and verbs.

REMEMBER WHEN...

Tuttle is a very old turtle. He likes to remember the past. Most of all, he enjoys remembering the weather. Tuttle always likes to tell the younger turtles stories about the weather.

Finish these sentences for Tuttle. Add the past tense form of the verb given after each sentence.

1. About fifty years ago, we _____ a terrible storm. **have**

2. Day after day, the rain _____ down. **pour**

3. The ground _____ wet and muddy. **become**

4. All that rain _____ everybody gloomy. **make**

5. After several weeks, the sun finally _____ out again. **come**

6. We all _____ thankful. **feel**

7. Then, about thirty-five years ago, a drought _____ . **strike**

8. The rivers and streams _____ up. **dry**

9. The plants _____ brown and wilted. **grow**

10. A hot, dry wind _____ . **blow**

11. We all _____ the sky for dark clouds. **watch**

12. At last, a gentle rain _____ . **fall**

13. I _____ you these weather stories last week. **tell**

14. Most of you _____ them the very next day. **forget**

Well, what happened next?

Birdseye Writing Skills: Sentences copyright © 1983 Pitman Learning, Inc.

Skill: Making past tense verb forms.

BIRDSEYE IN THE AIR

Early each evening, Birdseye likes to fly slowly through her neighborhood. She enjoys seeing what her neighbors do and hearing what they say, too.

Finish each of these sentences. Add the present tense verb that agrees with the sentence subject. Choose from the two verbs given after each sentence.

1. Birdseye _____ close to the ground.   **fly / flies**

2. Often, she _____ one wing to her friends.   **dip / dips**

3. On most evenings, she _____ the same people.   **see / sees**

4. Mr. and Mrs. Wagg _____ on their front porch.   **sit / sits**

5. They _____ quietly together.   **talk / talks**

6. Ollie and his sister often _____ ball on the front lawn.   **play / plays**

7. Sometimes Ollie's big dog and the puppy _____ the ball, too.   **chase / chases**

8. Ollie usually _____ to Birdseye.   **wave / waves**

9. Down the street, two girls _____ a jump rope.   **turn / turns**

10. Their friend _____ quickly over the rope.   **skip / skips.**

11. A group of older boys _____ on a car.   **work / works**

12. Families often _____ in the park.   **picnic / picnics**

13. Ms. Matchett and her sister _____ a barbecue.   **light / lights**

14. Hamburgers and hot dogs _____ on the grill.   **sizzle / sizzles**

What do some of your neighbors enjoy doing? _____

_____

Skill: Choosing present tense verbs (verb-subject agreement).

SOMETHING IN COMMON

Birdseye has many different friends, and she likes them all to get to know one another. Sometimes she has trouble convincing her friends that they have something in common.

Finish these sentences about Birdseye's friends. There are two verb forms given at the end of each sentence. First, circle the letter of the present tense verb that agrees with the sentence subject. Then write that verb in the blank space. The first one is completed.

1. Humpty Dumpty _____*sits*_____ on top of a high wall.   **g**-sit ⓐ-sits

2. He _____ back and forth.   **g**-teeters   **e**-teeter

3. Finally, he _____ off the wall.   **r**-tumbles   **t**-tumble

4. Two huge cracks _____ in his shell.
   e-appear   **i**-appears

5. A ripe apple _____ high up in a tree.   **a**-hangs   **h**-hang

6. The apple's stem _____ weaker and weaker.
   q-grow   **t**-grows

7. One warm day, the apple _____ to the ground.
   f-drops   **u**-drop

8. The players on a football team _____ well in every game.
   a-score   **e**-scores

9. The other teams in the league _____.   **k**-loses   **l**-lose

10. The football team _____ the championship.
    l-wins   **m**-win

In the boxes below, write the letters you circled from the sentences above. What do Humpty Dumpty, the ripe apple, and the championship team have in common?

Each one had ☐ ☐ ☐ ☐ ☐ ☐ ☐ ☐ ☐ ☐
              1   2 3 4 5 6   7 8 9 10

Skill: Choosing present tense verbs (verb-subject agreement).

THE BE BEE

This buzzing bee is really a verb we use often — the verb **be**. It has many hidden forms. Sometimes we use **be** as **am** or **is** or **are**. And sometimes we use **be** as **was** or **were**.

Finish these sentences by adding one of the verb forms given at the end of the sentence.

1. Yesterday, all the bees _____ in their hive.   **was / were**

2. A few bees _____ guarding the hive.   **was / were**

3. The others _____ safely inside.   **was / were**

4. They _____ watching a messenger bee.   **was / were**

5. That bee _____ doing a special dance.   **are / is**

6. It _____ about some fresh flowers that the bee has found.   **am / is**

7. I _____ sitting nearby, watching the hive.   **am / are**

8. The bees _____ very excited.   **am / are**

9. Now the hive _____ almost empty.   **am / is**

10. Most of the bees _____ gone.   **am / are**

11. They _____ gathering pollen from the flowers.   **are / is**

12. The flowers _____ bright and beautiful.   **am / are**

13. Each bee _____ buzzing from flower to flower.   **am / is**

14. I _____ very interested in bees.   **am / is**

Where's the honey?

Birdseye Writing Skills: Sentences copyright © 1983 Pitman Learning, Inc.

Skill: Choosing forms of the verb "be."

MORE PETS FOR PENELOPE

Penelope's collection of pets seems to grow and grow. She and her animals always have a good time together, but sometimes Penelope's pets get into trouble.

Finish each sentence by adding one of the verb forms given at the end of the sentence.

1. Some of Penelope's pets _____ very well behaved. **isn't/aren't**

2. They _____ always obey her. **doesn't/don't**

3. Most of her pets _____ stay off the furniture. **doesn't/don't**

4. Her biggest dog _____ been to obedience school. **hasn't/haven't**

5. Bowser _____ as quiet as he should be. **isn't/aren't**

6. Sometimes Penelope's neighbors _____ very happy about Bowser. **isn't/aren't**

7. Penelope _____ like to annoy her neighbors. **doesn't/don't**

8. Most of Penelope's cats _____ noisy. **isn't/aren't**

9. However, they _____ very friendly, either. **isn't/aren't**

10. Even Penelope's three goldfish _____ trouble-free. **isn't/aren't**

11. One of the fish _____ seem to like the water. **doesn't/don't**

12. Luckily, the cats _____ found the fish when he has jumped out of his bowl. **hasn't/haven't**

13. Penelope _____ unhappy with her pets, though. **isn't/aren't**

14. They _____ make her angry. **doesn't/don't**

Birdseye Writing Skills: Sentences copyright © 1983 Pitman Learning, Inc.

Skill: Choosing contraction verb forms (verb-subject agreement).

DONNIE DOUBLE

Donnie Double always does two things at once. When Donnie's friends sing, Donnie sings and dances. When his friends ride their bikes, Donnie rides his bike and claps his hands. Donnie also like sentences with compound predicates. This type of sentence has two predicates joined by a conjunction — **and**, **but**, or **or**.

Help Donnie Double find the sentences he likes. Underline each sentence that has a compound predicate.

1. Donnie is taking a special art class.

2. Usually the students paint or work with clay.

3. Yesterday, they made their own clay.

4. Donnie's partner mixed the flour with the salt and stirred in some water.

5. Donnie sprinkled in some more water and added a few drops of red food coloring.

6. He rolled a long piece of clay and then coiled it.

7. Donnie tried to make a tall tower.

8. The tower stood up well at first but then collapsed.

9. The teacher looked at Donnie's tower and made a few suggestions.

10. Donnie should make a wider tower or use a stronger coil of clay.

11. Donnie nodded and tried again.

12. He made a thick coil and then rolled it thinner at one end.

13. Donnie's partner helped him form a new tower.

14. The new tower grew quite tall and did not fall over.

15. Donnie let the tower dry and then took it home.

16. Donnie felt proud of his art project and showed it to everyone.

Birdseye Writing Skills: Sentences copyright © 1983 Pitman Learning, Inc.

Skill: Identifying compound predicates.

DONNIE AND MS. MATCHETT

Since Donnie Double likes sentences with compound predicates, Ms. Matchett is letting him use the Sentence Squeezer. Together, Donnie and Ms. Matchett have programmed the machine to make sentences with compound predicates.

Read each pair of sentences and run them through the Sentence Squeezer. Then write the new sentences that the Sentence Squeezer makes. Join the two predicates in each sentence with **and** or **but**.

1. We went to the horse show. We saw some beautiful ponies.

   _____

   _____

2. The trainers talked to the horses. The trainers patted them kindly.

   _____

   _____

3. One horse trotted into the ring. That horse performed several tricks.

   _____

   _____

4. The famous horse stood on his hind legs. The famous horse whinnied.

   _____

   _____

5. Each horse leaped over a fence. Each horse galloped smoothly away.

   _____

   _____

6. Those tricks look easy. Those tricks are actually quite difficult.

   _____

   _____

Skill: Combining sentences using compound predicates.

PICNIC TIME

Birdseye and her friends are getting ready for a picnic. It is a big job, and everyone must do two tasks. Look at each pair of pictures. Fill in the blanks to finish the sentences. Each of your sentences will have a compound predicate.

1. Birdseye _____

   and _____.

2. Ms. Matchett _____

   and _____.

3. Poor Carla _____

   but _____.

4. Birdseye's friend Ollie _____

   and _____.

Skill: Adding compound predicates.

MUMBLING MILTON

Milton has trouble making up his mind. He hates to express an opinion. If Milton sees a dog, for example, he has trouble deciding whether it is a big dog or a little dog, a friendly dog or an unfriendly dog. He doesn't know what *adjective* to use. So Milton mumbles, "That's a very mmmmm dog."

Help Milton make up his mind. Write an adjective above each set of Milton's mumbles.

1. That mmmmm dog jumped over the mmmmm fence.

2. Edgar took a mmmmm picture of the mmmmm waterfall.

3. Mia likes mmmmm music, but Reg prefers mmmmm music.

4. Only one mmmmm person saw the mmmmm shadow moving down the mmmmm street.

5. A mmmmm noise made all the mmmmm students sit up straight and look around.

6. Mmmmm ants and a mmmmm spider crawled in the mmmmm attic corner.

7. You can buy a mmmmm fish, a mmmmm snake, or a mmmmm kitten at that mmmmm pet store.

8. It was either a mmmmm story or a mmmmm lie.

9. The mmmmm hikers stopped for a mmmmm rest on the mountaintop.

10. The mmmmm machine suggested some mmmmm solutions to our mmmmm problems.

11. That mmmmm building must be the mmmmm library.

12. Two squirrels scrambled up the mmmmm tree.

Skill: Identifying adjectives.

FLYING WITH FIONA

Fiona loves to fly. She loves to talk about flying, too. Here are some sentences about one of Fiona's flights.

Expand each sentence by adding the adjective given after the sentence. The first sentence has been done for you.

1. My partner and I own a plane. (small)

   My partner and I own a small plane.

2. We had a trip recently. (unforgettable)

   _____

3. Before we started, we checked with the weatherman. (friendly)

   _____

4. We took off into the sky. (cloudless)

   _____

5. At first, we had a smooth flight. (comfortable)

   _____

6. My partner did some tricks with the plane. (difficult)

   _____

7. We made several turns. (tight)

   _____

8. Suddenly, a wind came up. (strong)

   _____

9. We could hardly control our plane. (light)

   _____

10. Finally, we landed the plane in a field. (flat)

    _____

Skill: Using adjectives to expand sentences.

Birdseye Writing Skills: Sentences copyright © 1983 Pitman Learning, Inc.

BORING BORIS

It's sad but true that Boris is boring. Whenever Boris speaks or writes, his sentences make sense, but they just aren't interesting. One problem is that Boris doesn't use enough adjectives in his sentences.

You and Birdseye can help Boris be less boring. Birdseye has left her prints in Boris' sentences. Every print marks a place where an adjective might be added. Make these sentences interesting by adding different adjectives. Write the new sentences.

1. One ⟑ day, my ⟑ friend and I decided to go sledding.

   _____

2. We dragged our ⟑ sleds to the ⟑ hill.

   _____

3. We saw ⟑ people there with ⟑ sleds and ⟑ toboggans.

   _____

4. One ⟑ girl showed us the ⟑ trail to the top.

   _____

5. The trail led up past ⟑ trees and ⟑ rocks.

   _____

6. We both got onto our ⟑ sleds and began the ⟑ trip down.

   _____

7. In the middle of the ⟑ hill, we hit a ⟑ patch of ⟑ ice.

   _____

8. Our sleds flew through the air, and we landed with ⟑ thuds in the ⟑ snow.

   _____

   _____

I'm not sure I'm ready to try this.

Birdseye Writing Skills: Sentences copyright © 1983 Pitman Learning, Inc.

Skill: Adding adjectives to expand sentences.

A SURPRISING VISITOR

Birdseye and her friends like to get together and talk about strange events. One evening, while they were talking, something strange happened to them. A gorilla walked in and surprised them.

Read each sentence. Find the word that tells **how** someone did something or **how** something happened. Circle that *adverb*, as in the first sentence.

1. Birdseye and her friends were talking (happily.)

2. Suddenly, the door to the room opened.

3. A huge, dangerous-looking gorilla entered the room noisily.

4. He stared violently at everyone in the room.

5. "I'm sleepy," the gorilla announced roughly.

6. Birdseye and her friends looked anxiously at one another.

7. Timidly, Birdseye spoke to the gorilla.

8. Quietly, he whispered his answer to Birdseye.

9. Birdseye took the gorilla's hand kindly and led him out of the room.

10. When Birdseye came back, her friends questioned her eagerly.

11. Birdseye shook her head wisely and said nothing.

Birdseye took the gorilla to the best bedroom in the house. She knows something special about big gorillas. What does Birdseye know?

Match the number under each box with the sentence numbers. In the box, write the first letter of the word you circled in that sentence.

A huge gorilla gets to sleep

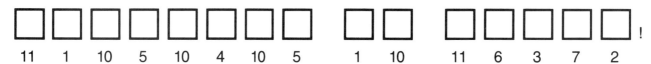

11	1	10	5	10	4	10	5	1	10	11	6	3	7	2	!

Birdseye Writing Skills: Sentences copyright © 1983 Pitman Learning, Inc.

Skill: Identifying adverbs.

A NEW GO-CART

Tillie and Tweezle like to build things. They have learned that sometimes they need to examine the things they built and make changes.

Expand and improve these sentences by adding adverbs, as in the first sentence. Using the adverbs given after each sentence, write the expanded sentence.

1. Tillie and Tweezle found an old wooden crate.   (yesterday)

   Tillie and Tweezle found an old wooden crate yesterday.

2. Tillie had an idea.   (suddenly)

   _____

3. She explained her idea to Tweezle.   (quickly)

   _____

4. Tillie and Tweezle dragged the old crate.   (home)

   _____

5. They collected wheels from old roller skates.   (together)

   _____

6. They attached the wheels to the crate.   (carefully)

   _____

7. Tillie and Tweezle searched the garage.   (thoroughly)

   _____

8. They found a good steering wheel.   (finally)

   _____

9. They showed the finished cart to their friends.   (proudly)

   _____

10. Tillie and Tweezle might enter their cart in a derby.   (soon)

    _____

Skill: Using adverbs to expand sentences.

BORIS RUNS A RACE

Boris jogs every day. Whenever he can, he also runs in races. Last weekend, Boris almost won a very exciting race. When he told his friends about the race, it did not seem very exciting, because Boris did not use adverbs.

Make Boris' sentences more interesting by adding adverbs to them. Birdseye has given you hints by leaving a print in each place where an adverb might be added. Write the new sentences.

1. All the runners crouched ✎ before the race began.

_____

2. I stretched my legs ✎.

_____

3. Miss Bricker clapped ✎ to signal the beginning of the race.

_____

4. ✎ I took the lead in the race.

_____

5. The fans cheered ✎.

_____

6. I dashed ✎ toward the finish line.

_____

7. ✎ I heard somebody behind me.

_____

8. ✎ I turned to look over my shoulder.

_____

9. Kristie smiled ✎ and raced past me.

_____

10. At the finish line, I congratulated her ✎ .

_____

Skill: Adding adverbs to expand sentences.

Birdseye Writing Skills: Sentences copyright © 1983 Pitman Learning, Inc.

ABOUT MERTON

My cat is lying **beside** me.

Meet Merton. He's sitting in his favorite chair. Whenever Merton talks, he uses *prepositions* in his sentences.

Finish these sentences for Merton. Add a preposition in each blank space. Use as many different prepositions as you can.

Prepositions: on, beside, through, in, out, at, with, around, about, to, for.

1. I like to stay _____ home _____ my cat.

2. Usually, everything _____ our house is very quiet.

3. Once, though, my friend Carlton pounded _____ the door.

4. Carlton looked very excited _____ something, and he was waving an envelope _____ one hand.

5. "Look _____ this!" he shouted.

6. "I have just won two tickets _____ Paris," Carlton explained, "and I want you to come _____ me."

7. Next day, I packed my bags and rushed _____ the airport.

8. Carlton and I stood _____ line _____ a long time before we could get _____ our plane.

9. We sat down _____ our assigned seats and looked _____ the window.

10. _____ the flight, Carlton and I ate two meals, watched a movie, and talked _____ the other passengers.

11. When the plane landed _____ Paris, Carlton and I took a cab _____ our hotel.

12. The next week, we walked _____ the river, ate _____ little cafés, strolled _____ famous museums, and shopped _____ the beautiful stores _____ Paris.

BIRDSEYE'S DIARY

Every day, Birdseye makes a new friend, has an adventure, or enjoys a favorite activity. Birdseye doesn't want to forget anything that has happened to her. So every evening, she writes in her diary. One evening Birdseye couldn't find her diary.

Read these sentences, and circle each prepositional phrase, as in the first sentence.

1. (After dinner,) Birdseye searched (for the diary.)

2. She usually keeps it in the top drawer of her desk.

3. Birdseye looked in each drawer, but the diary wasn't there.

4. Next, Birdseye looked on the table, on the couch in the living room, and even in the fireplace.

5. Birdseye searched for her diary in every corner of the kitchen.

6. Then Birdseye started looking under things.

7. She looked under the table, under the couch, under her desk, and even under the sink.

8. In each place, poor Birdseye found nothing.

9. Feeling very discouraged, Birdseye went to bed.

10. First, Birdseye looked under the bed for her diary.

11. There was nothing there, so she climbed into bed.

12. Birdseye's wing hit something hard in the bed.

13. She reached under the covers and found her favorite fountain pen.

14. Then Birdseye remembered that she had written in her diary while she was in bed, and finally she knew where to look.

Where do you think Birdseye found her diary?

_____

Birdseye Writing Skills: Sentences copyright © 1983 Pitman Learning, Inc.

Skill: Identifying prepositional phrases.

DOWN THE RIVER

Delilah was very excited about her raft trip. When she told her friends about it, Delilah wanted to include plenty of details. She wanted to use prepositional phrases in all her sentences.

Write each sentence the way Delilah would like it. Choose the prepositional phrase from the groups of words in parentheses.

1. We rode a raft (down the river, last Saturday).

   _____

2. The leader (of our group, and her friend) steered our raft.

   _____

3. We relaxed (and watched the river, in the raft).

   _____

4. Sometimes the rough water splashed (into our raft, the people).

   _____

5. (Finally, At noon) we stopped for lunch.

   _____

6. We heated our soup (and unwrapped sandwiches, over a fire).

   _____

7. We sat (quietly, on the shore) and ate.

   _____

8. (Much later, After lunch) we continued our raft trip.

   _____

9. We saw several deer (near the river, and many squirrels).

   _____

10. Everyone had fun (that day, on the raft trip).

    _____

Skill: Using prepositional phrases to expand sentences.

LITTLE BEANIE

Ms. Matchett loves using her Sentence Squeezer to combine sentences. The sentences she likes most are compound sentences — two whole sentences joined by the conjunction **and**, **but**, or **or**.

Help Ms. Matchett find her favorite kinds of sentences. Underline each compound sentence.

1. My sister Beanie has a new hobby, and it isn't easy to put up with.

2. She has started a collection of riddles.

3. Her collection has grown quickly, and she can't remember most of the riddles.

4. Beanie knows how most of the riddles begin, but she doesn't remember how they end.

5. We all try to be very patient with Beanie.

6. Dad usually whistles quietly, or he may tap his foot.

7. I know the answers to the riddles, but I'm not allowed to tell Beanie.

8. Actually, I don't want to hurt her feelings.

9. Most of Beanie's riddles aren't very funny, but we laugh anyway.

10. Yesterday, Beanie found a book of dinosaur riddles in the library.

11. She read the book carefully, and she even took notes.

12. Beanie liked most of the riddles, but she didn't understand all of them.

13. After dinner, she tried some of her new riddles out on me.

14. I had heard most of her riddles before, but one surprised me.

15. Beanie asked, "What do you call the dinosaur that puts bands on the teeth of other dinosaurs?"

Isn't that an orthodontosaurus?

Birdseye Writing Skills: Sentences copyright © 1983 Pitman Learning, Inc.

Skill: Identifying compound sentences.

MARVELLO THE MAGICIAN

Birdseye and her friends met Marvello the Magician. Ms. Matchett showed Marvello her new machine, the Sentence Squeezer. He was so impressed, he thought it must be magic!

Help Marvello use the Sentence Squeezer. Run each pair of sentences through the machine, and make a compound sentence with the conjunction **and**. The first pair has been combined for you already.

1. The newspaper told about Marvello. Birdseye wanted to see his show.

   The newspaper told about Marvello, and Birdseye wanted to see the show.

2. Birdseye told her friends about the show. They wanted to go, too.

   _____

3. Ollie talked to a ticket agent. She sold him eight tickets.

   _____

4. Marvello walked onto the stage. Everyone clapped for him.

   _____

5. The magician reached up his sleeve. A bright red scarf appeared.

   _____

6. He took off his hat. Three rabbits jumped out of it.

   _____

7. Then Marvello snapped his fingers. The rabbits disappeared.

   _____

8. Marvello asked for a volunteer. Birdseye jumped onto the stage.

   _____

9. Birdseye climbed into a special box. The assistant closed the lid.

   _____

Skill: Making compound sentences.

BIRDSEYE ON STAGE

Name _____

Marvello likes the Sentence Squeezer so much that he may start using it in his magic show. He has decided that Birdseye can help him run the machine, but she isn't ready to appear in his show.

Help Birdseye and Marvello use the Sentence Squeezer. Run each pair of sentences through the machine, and make a compound sentence. Choose the best conjunction — **and**, **but**, or **or**.

1. Birdseye enjoyed the show. She decided to do some magic tricks.

   _____

2. Birdseye tried her first trick. It was not very successful.

   _____

3. She reached up her sleeve. Nothing was there.

   _____

4. Then she looked inside her hat. Nothing was there either.

   _____

5. Birdseye's friends were surprised. They didn't laugh at her.

   _____

6. Birdseye could have read books about magic. She might have talked with

   Marvello. _____

   _____

7. Birdseye felt embarrassed. She tried one more trick.

   _____

8. She snapped her fingers. Finally something happened.

   _____

9. Birdseye disappeared. Nobody could find her.

   _____

Birdseye Writing Skills: Sentences copyright © 1983 Pitman Learning, Inc.

Skill: Making compound sentences.

ANSWER KEY

Hidden Treasure, page 1
2., 3., 6., 7., 8., 12., and 14.
It was Scamp's collection of buried bones.

Bonnie and Her Boxes, page 2
statements: 1., 5., 10.   commands: 3., 6., 12.
questions: 4., 7., 8.   exclamations: 2., 9., 11.

Birdseye's Friends at Work, page 3
1. statement
2. command
3. exclamation
4. question
5. question
6. exclamation
7. statement
8. command
9. exclamation
10. statement
11. statement
12. question
13. command
14. question

Wandering Woody, page 4
1. question mark
2. period or exclamation point
3. period or exclamation point
4. question mark
5. period or exclamation point
6. question mark
7. period or exclamation point
8. question mark
9. period or exclamation point
10. period
11. period
12. period
13. question mark
14. period or exclamation point

Picking Up the Pieces, page 5
1. I love to play baseball.
2. I play on a team called the Sluggers.
3. The Sluggers will win the championship this season.
4. Do you like to play baseball?
5. What position do you play?
6. Would you like to practice with us?
7. Watch the ball.
8. Hit it as hard as you can.
9. What a great hit that was!
10. You should join the Sluggers!

At the Beach, page 6
Answers will vary.

Spelunking with Spencer, page 7
1. a.1   4. a.1   7. b.2
2. s.5   5. l.3   8. a.1
3. m.4   6. l.3   9. t.6

a		s	m	a	l	l		b	a	t
1		2	3	4	5	6		7	8	9

Welcome to the Zoo, page 8
Approximate answers:
1. Elephants
2. Monkeys
3. Seals
4. Snakes
5. Ostriches
6. Crocodiles
7. Owls

The Noun-Napper, page 9
Answers will vary.

Ollie Outdo, page 10
1. brothers
2. sisters
3. mice
4. butterflies
5. guppies
6. friends
7. rosebushes
8. ideas
9. libraries
10. countries
11. movies
12. peaches
13. women
14. watches

Polly Parrot, page 11
1. They lost their famous diamond.
2. She was asked to solve the mystery.
3. He was assigned to help her.
4. It was a very difficult assignment.
5. They were hard to understand.
6. It was extremely valuable.
7. They worked very hard.
8. We could have helped them solve the case.

Tillie and Tweezle, page 12
1., 3., 6., 8., 10., 11., 13., 15.

Ms. Matchett's Machine, page 13
1. Lottie and her friends went camping.
2. Lottie and Doreen pitched the tent.
3. Jan and Nina gathered wood for the campfire.
4. Anya and her mother started cooking dinner.
5. The hamburgers and (the) roasted marshmallows tasted great.
6. The tall mountains and (the) clear lakes were beautiful.
7. Beth and Peter wanted to go hiking.
8. Tom and Heidi went fishing instead of hiking.

Birdseye's Special Circus, page 14
1. A bear and a monkey
2. A monkey and a clown
3. A lion and a tiger
4. A boy and a girl
5. Bo and Jo
6. A cat and a dog

Penelope's Pets, page 15
1. is one of Penelope's favorite pets.
2. felt sick one day.
3. looked pale.
4. drooped.
5. wanted to help her sick duck.
6. wouldn't take care of Penelope's duck.
7. called a quack instead.
8. has a pet frog, too.
9. is an excellent jumper.
10. can jump higher than the Empire State Building.
11. can't jump very high at all.
12. is a big watchdog.
13. has trained her dog very carefully.
14. still runs around in circles, though.
15. must be trying to wind itself up.

Sports Confusion, page 16
1. All the players on our team ran onto the playing field.
2. The coach shouted to the players.
3. The soccer game started at noon.
4. The people in the stands cheered for the players after the game.
5. A big bulldog acted as our team mascot.
6. The goalie from the other team blocked every kick.

A Surprise Party, page 17
Approximate answers:
1. Lupe wrote invitations.
2. Her brother mailed the invitations.
3. Lupe decorated the living room.
4. Diego frosted the birthday cake.
5. All the guests jumped out of their hiding places.
6. Their mother was surprised.

Lazy Leona, page 18
1. rises
2. stay
3. walk
4. talk
5. lie
6. ends
7. move
8. chatter
9. stroll
10. flies
11. munches
12. trot

r e s t
1 6 2 4

Best Friends, page 19
1. star—N, star—V
2. pedal—V, pedal—N
3. lights—V, lights—N
4. sign—N, sign—V
5. cheer—N, cheer—V
6. dress—V, dress—N

More Disagreements, page 20
1. wave—V, wave—N
2. step—V, step—N
3. fish—N, fish—V
4. time—V, time—N
5. form—N, form—V
6. store—N, store—V

Remember When, page 21
1. had
2. poured
3. became
4. made
5. came
6. felt
7. struck
8. dried
9. grew
10. blew
11. watched
12. fell
13. told
14. forgot

Birdseye in the Air, page 22
1. flies
2. dips
3. sees
4. sit
5. talk
6. play
7. chase
8. waves
9. turn
10. skips
11. works
12. picnic
13. light
14. sizzle

Something in Common, page 23
1. sits
2. teeters
3. tumbles
4. appear
5. hangs
6. grows
7. drops
8. score
9. lose
10. wins

a   g r e a t   f a l l
1   2 3 4 5 6   7 8 9 10

The Be Bee, page 24
1. were
2. were
3. were
4. were
5. is
6. is
7. am
8. are
9. is
10. are
11. are
12. are
13. is
14. am

More Pets for Penelope, page 25
1. aren't
2. don't
3. don't
4. hasn't
5. isn't
6. aren't
7. doesn't
8. aren't
9. aren't
10. aren't
11. doesn't
12. haven't
13. isn't
14. don't

Donnie Double, page 26
compound predicates in 2., 4., 5., 6., 8., 9., 10., 11., 12., 14., 15., 16.

Donnie and Ms. Matchett, page 27
1. We went to the horse show and saw some beautiful ponies.
2. The trainers talked to the horses and patted them kindly.
3. One horse trotted into the ring and performed several tricks.
4. The famous horse stood on his hind legs and whinnied.
5. Each horse leaped over a fence and galloped smoothly away.
6. Those tricks look easy but are actually quite difficult.

Picnic Time, page 28
Approximate answers:
1. Birdseye makes sandwiches and wraps them up.
2. Ms. Matchett boils eggs and peels them.
3. Poor Carla tries to open a jar of pickles but drops it.
4. Birdseye's friend Ollie cuts up vegetables and makes a salad.

Mumbling Milton, page 29
Answers will vary.

Flying with Fiona, page 30
2. We had an unforgettable trip recently.
3. Before we started, we checked with the friendly weatherman.
4. We took off into the cloudless sky.
5. At first, we had a smooth, comfortable flight.
6. My partner did some difficult tricks with the plane.
7. We made several tight turns.
8. Suddenly, a strong wind came up.
9. We could hardly control our light plane.
10. Finally, we landed the plane in a flat field.

Boring Boris, page 31
Answers will vary.

A Surprising Visitor, page 32
2. Suddenly
3. noisily
4. violently
5. roughly
6. anxiously
7. Timidly
8. Quietly
9. kindly
10. eagerly
11. wisely

w h e r e v e r   h e   w a n t s !
11 1 10 5 10 4 10 5   1 10   11 6 3 7 2

A New Go-Cart, page 33
(Adverb placement may vary.)
2. Suddenly, Tillie had an idea.
3. She quickly explained her idea to Tweezle.
4. Tillie and Tweezle dragged the old crate home.
5. Together, they collected wheels from old roller skates.
6. They carefully attached the wheels to the crate.
7. Tillie and Tweezle thoroughly searched the garage.
8. They finally found a steering wheel.
9. They proudly showed the finished cart to their friends.
10. Tillie and Tweezle might enter their cart in a derby soon.

Boris Runs a Race, page 34
Answers will vary.

About Merton, page 35
(Some answers may vary.)
1. at/with
2. around
3. on
4. about/in
5. at
6. to/with
7. to
8. in/for/on
9. in/out
10. During/to
11. in/to
12. beside/at/through/in/ around

Birdseye's Diary, page 36
2. in the top drawer/of her desk
3. in each drawer
4. on the table/on the couch/in the living room/in the fireplace
5. for her diary/in every corner/of the kitchen
6. under things
7. under the table/under the couch/under her desk/under the sink
8. In each place
9. to bed
10. under the bed/for her diary
11. into bed
12. in the bed
13. under the covers
14. in her diary/in bed

Down the River, page 37
1. down the river
2. of our group
3. in the raft
4. into our raft
5. At noon
6. over a fire
7. on the shore
8. After lunch
9. near the river
10. on the raft trip

Little Beanie, page 38
compound sentences are: 1., 3., 4., 6., 7., 9., 11., 12., 14.

Marvello the Magician, page 39
2. Birdseye told her friends about the show, and they wanted to go, too.
3. Ollie talked to a ticket agent, and she sold him eight tickets.
4. Marvello walked onto the stage, and everyone clapped for him.
5. The magician reached up his sleeve, and a bright red scarf appeared.
6. He took off his hat, and three rabbits jumped out of it.
7. Then Marvello snapped his fingers, and the rabbits disappeared.
8. Marvello asked for a volunteer, and Birdseye jumped onto the stage.
9. Birdseye climbed into a special box, and the assistant closed the lid.

Birdseye on Stage, page 40
1. Birdseye enjoyed the show, and she decided to do some magic tricks.
2. Birdseye tried her first trick, but it was not very successful.
3. She reached up her sleeve, but nothing was there.
4. Then she looked inside her hat, but nothing was there either.
5. Birdseye's friends were surprised, but they didn't laugh at her.
6. Birdseye could have read books about magic, or she might have talked with Marvello.
7. Birdseye felt embarrassed, but she tried one more trick.
8. She snapped her fingers, and finally something happened.
9. Birdseye disappeared, and nobody could find her.